WOMEN
OF OLD WHO
PRAYED

The Contemporary Woman's
Guide to Prayer...

Mavis A.S. Agyemang

ACKNOWLEDGEMENTS

My gratitude to the Holy Spirit for the inspiration to write yet another book.

Special thanks to Bernard and Eugene, my publishing consultants at BKC Consulting.

CONTENTS

*Acknowledgement*______________________________*iii*
*Introduction*______________________________*v*

Chapter 1: Hagar______________________________1
Chapter 2: The Daughters of Zelophehad__13
Chapter 3: Naomi______________________________23
Chapter 4: Esther______________________________33
Chapter 5: Hannah______________________________45
Chapter 6: Anna______________________________57
Chapter 7: The Canaanite Woman______67

*About the Author*______________________________77

INTRODUCTION

When James wanted to encourage the early Believers regarding their personal relationship with God and to boost their faith in their prayer, he wrote to them, *"Elijah was a man with a nature like ours, and he prayed fervently that it might not rain, and for three years and six months it did not rain on the earth"* (James 5:17). James didn't want the first century church to assume that they needed to be extraordinary human beings with special characteristics to have a relationship with God and to qualify to be heard by Him.

Like those early Christians, many of us today tend to believe that the Believers of old were superhuman. We assume that, for figures like Elijah to call down fire, shut up rains in the heavens and release it by their prayer, there must be something remarkable about them. But now, from the scripture above, we understand that Bible characters like Abraham, or Moses, or Deborah, or David, or Daniel are just as human as we are and have been so from Adam to Paul. Neither has their circumstances changed than ours. They suffered some things for God, and so do we. They faced individual frustrations and struggles just as we do today.

Additionally, what this means is that, the criteria for relating to God hasn't changed *much*. In spite of all that God accomplished through figures such as Jochebed the mother of Moses, Miriam the sister of Moses, Deborah the warrior, the five daughters of

Zelophehad, Rahab the prostitute, Mary or Elisabeth, they were ordinary women—just like you, just like me. God hears and answers our prayers just as He did with those of old. The requirement remains righteousness and fervency for prayer to be effective.

For as many women who wrongly believe there is something extraordinary about the women of the Bible, this book is written. For as many women who do not understand the true background and circumstances of their Biblical counterparts, this book is written. For as many contemporary women who desire to model their lives after the women of old so as to also experience the hand of God in their lives, this book is written. ***Women of Old Who Prayed*** reintroduces to you a few women whose prayer became scripture, and whose names are mentioned wherever this gospel is preached.

Many women prayed during the days of the Bible. For instance, Miriam the brother of Moses; Deborah the only woman who rose to political authority in the Bible; and Elizabeth the mother of John the Baptist all prayed. Huldah was a prophetess in the Old Testament (2 Kings 22:14-20). She was outspoken like many of her male counterparts, and like them, she prophesied in the name of the Lord, *"Thus saith the Lord."* It is impossible for a female prophet like Huldah not to pray.

However, we are not privileged to have the contents of her prayer disclosed to us. We are fortunate, however, to have more prayers of women in the Bible than I intend to explore to achieve my purpose for writing this book. I have thus selected only seven of those women whose prayer is recorded, and delved briefly into their family background and history, their peculiar challenges or problems that drove them to seek God through prayer, how God came through for them and the lessons that all of these hold for us contemporary women.

By their conduct or way of life, the women talked about here teach us how to handle life issues relating to marriage and family life, childbearing, tragedy or disaster, finances, civil life, and our personal relationship with God. The book shows that these Bible characters are real human beings like ourselves, and who went through similar challenges as we do in our day, and cried or grieved over the same things that break our hearts.

This understanding would help us appreciate our relationship with God, and the opportunity we have to speak to Him as our Father by means of prayer.

CHAPTER 1

Hagar

Hagar—let's call her mother of the wild ass.

A young woman of Egyptian origin, Hagar was purchased by Sarah and Abraham during the time of their dwelling in Egypt. Her story is found in Genesis 16; 21:8–21.

As a maid, one could make certain simple assumptions about Hagar and be right about them. For instance, the maid she was, she certainly didn't have a voice of her own. Her opinions didn't really matter, so no one listened to her, paid attention to her, or tried to understand her. She didn't have her independence. She didn't have many liberties and rights—such as the right to choose what she wanted, the right to make her own decisions, the right to chase her own goals and dreams in life. In times when she needed defense, not even Abraham the father of her unborn child could stand up to her defense. She was merely living on the dictates of her mistress, whom she was obliged to obey when instructed by her. That is how come she could be instructed to sleep with Abraham—and whether it was against her wish or not didn't matter.

Though a believing family, though a family of faith, they could not understand or tame Hagar. This *"Christian family"* *"dealt harshly with her, and she fled."* In all these, God loved her and established a relationship with her.

We cannot blame Hagar for the mistake of Sarah in suggesting that Abraham *"go in to my maid; perhaps I shall obtain children by her"* (*Genesis 16:2*). God's intention was for Sarah to have a child by herself. If Hagar knew it, perhaps she would not have agreed to be surrogate mother for the promised child of Abraham and Sarah. As far as we know, we should stay away from people's covenanted life. But there are times we find ourselves in circumstances like Hagar did. A married man pretending to be single and luring another young woman to marry him or get pregnant for him can be an example.

Approached from another angle, it can be rightly observed also that Hagar was the rebellious maid who taught her mistress the bitter lesson of her life, and suffered the consequences of her actions by getting thrown out. Actions have consequences. As the recalcitrant maid, Hagar didn't play her cards well, and it went against her bitterly. She had a hidden bad character that manifested when she thought her circumstances had changed.

Many young people have turned and punished people who took them in as young sisters with good intentions. There are many people like Sarah who have need of other young people like Hagar but are afraid to reach out because they have been hurt, let down, and stabbed in the back. It would be difficult for someone in the shoes of Sarah to trust another person who needs the help of someone like Sarah in her life. We have to understand that when we let people down when they give us opportunities, we make it difficult for people who will need similar help in the future.

Whichever angle we approach the story from, as women, we can sometimes find ourselves in both circumstances—we are sometimes the unfortunate maid, and at other times, the rebellious maid. Yet whichever one we are in right now, we still would need to pray.

Hagar Teaches Rich Lessons

The story of Hagar teaches us a lot of lessons about offences and forgiveness, submission and obedience, and repentance. Here are some of them in more detail.

First, there are a few terrible things about Hagar that we must learn to eschew, if we are to avoid falling into circumstances like her. Hagar was an example of people who abuse opportunities, or people who take advantage of other people's kindness or vulnerability. She didn't have to start being disrespecting towards her mistress after being given the chance to become pregnant. There are times we behave like her. We develop bride and arrogance when we begin to rise in life and in our accomplishments. We also begin to take revenge on people we have secretly hated but didn't have the power to touch.

Another lesson is that, Hagar allowed herself to go through challenges before seeking the help of God. It is better to prevent than to cure. If we go wrong, we can be sure to get scolded or punished by God, but He will forgive and restore. It is up to us to seek forgiveness and restoration when we err. Hagar knew how to repent and seek God again. God's word to Hagar is God's word to us who are like her. Just as she obeyed and returned to the humble service of her mistress, we must be doers of the Word of God. But it is better that we do not get ourselves in circumstances that require God's chastening before restoring us.

Woman, You're Not Alone

Hagar and her son were alone in the wilderness. Sometimes, life can seem lonely. We live alone. We fight alone. We face our battles and problems alone. Hagar and her son found themselves in the lonely desert. But the angel of God appeared to them. I believe, dear woman, that God is with you in your alone moments. If you call upon Him when everyone else has deserted you, He will come through for you.

God Never Abandons Us

God is with us in all our troubles, afflictions and pain. He never abandons us. No, not in our worst offences or mistakes. Being abandoned by our employers, family, husbands, or friends does not equate to being abandoned by God, too. God sent His angel to Hagar and promised to bless her son, too (Genesis 16:7–14). Hagar thought she was lost. But the angel of the Lord found her (Genesis 16:7). We are not lost; we are not abandoned. God knows our whereabouts. He will find us. His angels are on guard. He is the Good Shepherd who finds the lost sheep. In Hagar's affliction, God took notice. God is not unaware of your circumstances. He is coming to your aid, having *"listened to your affliction."* Depend on God in times of hardship and difficulties. He sees, He knows, He hears. God provided for Hagar and Ishmael in the desert. He can and will provide for you too, dear woman. Learn to depend on God in times of need, and watch Him perform miracles in your life *(Genesis 21:8–21).*

Tears are Prayers too
It is not stated anywhere in the scripture that Hagar prayed. Both she and her son cried because of their affliction, and God heard their cry. Our tears, silent sobs, and unspeakable

desires we are trying to suppress are all known to God. Tears are a prayer too. It is alright to go through difficult things and cry. Like Hagar, God will come through for you and you will realize that God sees you *(Genesis 16:13)*.

"Power pass power"

Abraham gave Sarah his wife the authority and power over Hagar her maid, and she dealt with her *(Genesis 16:6)*. This shows that power is in ranks. We all do not wield the same amount of power. There are levels in every organization or setting. Some are senior to others. Those who are lower ranking like Hagar must learn to be submissive to those in higher authority like Sarah. Otherwise, we will face the same consequence as Hagar. Sarah showed Hagar where power lay.

Don't Invite Envy

From the point of view of those who are sympathetic to Hagar, thinking instead that, Sarah became jealous of her, we have to remember that jealousy or envy is real, but how we carry ourselves determines whether we will attract envy or love. I know it is impossible not to attract envy, but don't make people jealousy by reminding them of their plight.

Women Must Unite

Women must learn to live together and tolerate one another. It is popularly believed that we women are our own enemies. We hunt down one another, oppose one another and compete among ourselves. Dear woman, be not a partaker of these. Be a woman with a difference. Be a woman who loves, accommodates, is humble, patient and tolerant. Be the woman who supports another woman.

Share Your Experience of Jesus

Sarah and Abraham introduced Hagar to their God, Yahweh, the God of the Hebrews. We can say that they made every effort to raise young Hagar in the fear of the Lord. Hagar could now direct her tears to the Lord who will look on her with mercy, and bless her offspring. We ought to use every opportunity we have to tell others about Jesus and, invite them to Him. Remember to mention them before the Lord, and ask Him to draw the sinner to Himself.

Press on to Victory

Our present circumstances should not discourage us from fighting on in life. Although Hagar was broke, homeless, depressed and alone, she believed the promise of God was going to manifest in her life someday. Even if things were not in good shape, I hope she realized someday that it was all her fault for refusing to submit to authority, so that she doesn't repeat it. But I commend her for seeking God and pressing on. Today the promise by the angel who appeared to her is fulfilled.

CHAPTER 2

The Daughters of Zelophehad

Once upon a time, tithing was not a Biblical practice until Abraham introduced it and God *"sanctioned"* it. Once upon a time, Jacob wrestled with an angel who touched the socket of his hip on the sinew of the thigh and Jacob's hip was put out of joint and he limped in his walk, and *"to this day the people of Israel do not eat the sinew of the thigh that is on the hip socket"* (Genesis 32:32). Once upon a time, Esther led her people in exile to pray against an influential leader who plotted their destruction, and till today, the Purim Festival is marked yearly to celebrate the incidence. And once upon a time, Jewish women had no rights to own property until the daughters of Zelophehad marched to declare their property rights as women.

At a time when women were prohibited by national law from inheriting their fathers, a man by the name of Zelophehad dies leaving no sons as heirs to his properties. That was the provision in the Biblical law at the time; it restricted property inheritance to sons. Women could marry into other tribes and exchange landownerships.

Five women—without a father, and without brothers, yet they stood their ground and defended their faith and right. They respectfully approached authority and presented their petition. Zelophehad's daughters took their petition to Moses, the priest and elders of Israel because they believed their father's property belonged to them even though they didn't have brothers to inherit their fathers.

They were bold enough to challenge the law, norms and status quo! On that day, perhaps the first ever documented property inheritance lawsuit was filed. And from that day, the laws regarding inheritance was rewritten. Evidence of the amendment that has changed lives by bringing relief to so many women is found in Numbers 36:2-8. They claimed women's part of the promise—the Promised Land. Their fierce courage brought about women inheriting lands in the Promised Land too.

They presented their petition to God through Moses. Our first lesson is that, it is alright to request prayer support from our fellow Christians, pastors and spiritual leaders. Moses went before God on behalf of the women. Your pastor or fellowship leader or brother or sister in Christ can intercede for you in prayer. If you are under severe attack, reach out and ask for help in prayer.

Christian writer Courtney Joseph shares an insightful reflection on the story of the daughters of Zelophehad. She says, *"Sometimes I think we assume that once we are saved, blessings should just pour down from heaven on us. This is not the case. Sometimes blessings do not come until we have walked a painful road. Sometimes blessings do not come until we have prayed hard to God, begging for change. Sometimes blessings do not come until we step out in faith—way outside our comfort zone—and watch God work through us, despite our feeble selves. Sometimes blessings do not come until we gather the courage to confront something that is wrong, to make it right."*

Sometimes your prayer to God gets answered spiritually, but it is up to us to move in the physical to change the situation for our prayer to come to pass in real life. We serve a God who is full of compassion and miracles. He is ready to help us all.

Moses may never had thought along those lines. But when they presented their case, Moses realized it was a peculiar case and had to be taken before God. Our leaders do not know it all. Some things spring out of experience. If you have gone through an experience, it may be because God wants to bring about change through you concerning the experience.

When we fall into certain situations, or when God allows certain challenges our way, it is not with the intent to destroy us. You are not in that situation because God wants to punish you, but because He wants to accomplish something through you. God is waiting for you to take the step so that He will say, *"Yes, you are right, grant her the right!"* That day, the women's circumstance led to changing one of the laws of Israel till today.

There comes a time in life when we have no option than to do what has never been done before. Like the 4 lepers breaking the law and coming into the city because they were so hungry and about to die. Like Esther walking into the presence of the king unbidden. Like the people who, after a long time in American history, led protests after protests to get the courts to remove every barrier to African American suffrage and bring an end to denial of voting rights to African Americans. Today, step out boldly. You may be taking chances to change the course of history like the daughters of Zelophehad.

As women, we can take up the place of men. Most women think they cannot accomplish certain things because those things are in the domain of men. Hear me, dear woman, there is nothing a man can do that you cannot do. Stand up and take your place. Your husband or brothers may not be in the position to accomplish them, but you can rise up and do them.

What we fight for today or what we fight to build today can benefit thousands of generations after us. Your prayer request should be, "Dear God, help me leave a legacy for those coming after me"; "Help me to fight family battles once and for all." These ladies did not only fight for themselves, but they wanted to ensure that this trend didn't continue into the Promised Land. They advocated for reforms, women empowerment, and equality. They fought against discrimination against women.

Rachel Chung's words are encouraging for those tempted to think their input is insignificant: *"It's easy to become jaded, to feel like small actions won't actually help push a bill forward or advance an equal rights agenda….Mahlah, Noah, Hoglah, Milcah and Tirzah's action reminds us that sometimes, the simple act of raising your voice for what you believe is right does, indeed, make a difference."*

Truly, God listens when we pray. God declared support for the ladies. "The daughters of Zelophehad are right. You shall give them possession of an inheritance among their father's brothers and transfer the inheritance of their father to them" (Numbers 27:7). We have to understand that we have the support and backing of God. Once we are fighting a good cause or doing what is right, we can never be at enmity with God.

Finally, the women proved to be knowledgeable. They were *"learned"* enough to know the history of their family and nation, as well the nature of their laws. Silvina Chemen writes that, *"These women know their law and history. They use the fact that their father was not involved in Korach's rebellion (Numbers 16) as evidence to support his—and their—claim to the land. They know that the continuity of family name depends on inheritance of the land; and they realize that the current law is not adequate, for it does not take into account the unusual circumstances of a man without sons. They possess the acumen to recognize this omission—in God's law!"*

Women must be learners. It takes people with trained and educated minds to accomplish what the daughters of Zelophehad accomplished. The quest for knowledge must not die among women who desire to influence or change norms and status quos.

CHAPTER 3

Naomi

The story of Naomi is popular for the grief she suffered when she lost her husband and two children in a space of about 10 years as an expatriate in Moab, but which somewhat ended in joy. Famine breaks out in her country, Judah, compelling her and her entire family to move to Moab. But things take a sour turn. Her family is attacked by the demon of death, and within a twinkle of an eye, Naomi, the happily married woman and mother of two adult boys, is widowed and childless.

Another significant part of the Naomi story is the loyalty she enjoyed from her daughter-in-law, Ruth, who refused to abandon the poor old woman to her fate.

Naomi's life and story teaches us a great deal about life, faith, prayer, salvation, endurance, divine intervention, spiritual warfare, and the faithfulness of God in the midst of all our suffering. Her life teaches us that a bad beginning can make a good ending. Though our beginning was small, our end can be great. The glory of the latter life can be greater than the former.

At this turn of events in her life, like most of us would, Naomi is bitter about her predicament, and blames God for her troubles. We observe that, unlike Eli (1 Samuel 3:10–18) and Job (Job 2:9–10), Naomi is angry and hurt that her onetime wonderful life and family is gone, with all hopes of ever having a marriage or children again. She blames God for it all, and is angry and bitter toward Him.

When Naomi eventually decides to return to Bethlehem, her hometown, the events surrounding her departure is revealing of her true character and ministry. Her prayer ministry is brought to light. We learn that Naomi is a prayer warrior and a family intercessor. Before she dismissed her daughters-in-law, Naomi prayed for them, and pronounced blessings upon them. This is worthy of emulation. Although herself a widow, she prays for the younger widows, against the rising up of affliction again in their life. Mark McDowell writes that Naomi's *"first inclination is not to pray for herself, but for others. What a wonderful attitude to have in prayer."*

Why did Naomi Pray?

But why did Naomi pray—and what was her prayer request to God? From the account, we can learn that there are important people in our lives who need our intercession and on various occasions, we must pray for them. Naomi prayed because her family was under attack. She prayed for the younger generations of her family. Naomi teaches us that we must intercede for people and speak positively into their lives. From our children and relatives to our employees, friends and spiritual children. Knowing that there is power in the tongue, Naomi made positive declarations and pronouncements upon their life; she blessed, not curse.

Naomi also prayed because a time of departure had arrived. It was a time of parting ways with people in her life, a time to say goodbye. One of the critical times for prayer and intercession is departure times. There is a departure time for every family. Each morning, we depart to work, to school or to honour various appointments. We part to school or the boarding house, for vacation or for brief trips. All these require us to pray and keep each other in prayer. Family times of prayer before we leave home each day should not be missed. Apart from family, we also frequently part ways with people at church, friends, and colleague workers who are relocating. Departing times are occasions to celebrate and show appreciation to those who have been good to us over the years. Isaac blessed his son Jacob before sending him away to Laban his Uncle (Genesis 28:1–5). Laban blessed his grandchildren and children as they departed with their father, Jacob (Genesis 31:55). In Acts 20:36–38, Paul shares a solemn prayer with his friends and ministry associates and church members as he departs. We must send our departing parties away with the presence and blessing of the Lord.

Finally, Naomi prayed for her daughters-in-law because they had supported their husbands and just when they should be enjoying the fruits of their labour, they lost their husbands. She prayed for them because they had been good wives and good daughters-in-law. She shows us that we have to pray for and bless people who support us and who have been good to us—our friends and relatives, husbands, children, co-workers, fellow labourers in the Lord. You have to teach your children to pray for their mates—many of them support your children with their assignments, love, protect and keep them company; teach your children to pray for their teachers, for their spiritual leaders, for their parents and spouses when they marry.

Become Your Family Intercessor

Naomi is a family intercessor. She prays for relatives. She does not wish that what came upon her should come upon the generations after her. She prays and stops evil patterns—patterns of death, patterns of premature death, widowhood, marital failure, childlessness, generational curses.

Dear woman, I urge you to emulate the steps of Naomi. Make it your goal to pray for your family all the time. Below are prayer topics to pray for your family and friends.

- Pray the blessing of God upon your daughters—biological and spiritual. Pray for their future marriages and for the works of their hands;
- Pray for God to release the rewards of their labour. Pray for people they have helped to remember them as they do well in life;

- Pray that they will not go in full—to work or into a businesses or marriage, and return empty;
- Pray that they may find husbands, and good ones, and that they enjoy their marriages; pray that their faithfulness be rewarded;
- Pray for them to find peaceful marriages;
- Pray that their story will end well; pray that it will end well with them in everything they do;
- Break every curse upon their life in Jesus' name;
- Pray that God will give you people who give good guidance and Godly counsel. (It matters who advices you. It is important who you listen to. Who is your friend and who is your advisor? Who is your pastor?); Pray that God will bring you into contact with people who are wise and filled with the Holy Spirit to advise you; pray same for your children;

- Pray for God to bring loyal people into your life, and into the lives of your family members;
- Pray that like Naomi, Ruth and Orpha, God will make you a survivor and a remnant.
- Pray that the faith of your children will remain steadfast in the face of adversity, challenges, and hardships;
- Pray against bitterness in their life;
- Pray against their untimely death; pray that you do not have to bury them. *(Children should bury their parents and not the other way round).*
- Pray that God will wipe away their tears, and give them joy for their sorrow, beauty for their ashes, gladness for their mourning;
- Pray that they keep their faith in spite of anything that befalls them—in the face persecution, affliction, hardship, delay.
- Pray that God will bring loyal people into their lives who can

almost replace their dead—and replenish their losses.

- Pray for people who are going through hardships like Naomi and Ruth and Orpah. It is not easy to lose loved ones—husbands, children, parents, siblings, friends. Such people need our prayer.

God bless you.

CHAPTER 4

Esther

*"I will go to the king, though it is against the
law, and if I perish, I perish."*
—Esther 4:16, ESV

Esther, otherwise called Hadassah, was one of the greatest women prayer warriors of the Bible. Her story has a beautiful background to it. Esther rises to queenship following the removal from the throne of Queen Vashti at an extravagant party where she declined an order by her husband the the king to dance for him. In a fairy tale fashion, the king seeks counsel from his political advisors about this marital issue and is advised to *"give her royal position to another who is better than she"*

(Esther 1:19). After a beauty contest held for the purpose of selecting a new queen, Esther, a Jewess, emerged the new Queen of Persia—a foreign land.

Esther soon discovers that Haman, the second most powerful man in the Persian Kingdom, is the Jewish refugee community's most staunch hater, who is plotting an annihilation of them. As Haman's plot reaches an advanced stage, the Jews' counterplan, spearheaded by Mordecai, Esther's elderly cousin, receives the collective support of all members of the Jewish community. A fast is held among the Jews, and Esther takes the biggest risk of her life, actually risking her life in the course of it all. In the end, Haman's plot to massacre the Jews is overthrown, and Esther wins victory for her people, and till today, remains a heroine to her people. The first celebration of the Purim Festival was help to mark this deliverance, and has since been celebrated yearly every 14th and 15th March to today.

The Book of Esther in the Bible is unique for one thing: there is no mention of God and no prayer was said anywhere! Although this has become of source of controversy amongst scholars, God and the power of prayer are seen effectively working in the story. The book explains the origins of the celebration of the Feast of Purim, the festival that emerged and became institutionalized after the Jews escaped Hama's annihilation plot.

Although prayer and God are not spoken of in this book, we know that fasting goes with prayer. Debbie McDaniel submits that, *"Although we don't read God's name in the story, His sovereignty and loving care are woven throughout the words and chapters."*

Learning from Esther's Story

Esther's familiar story is woven around the events that dared a young queen to risk her life for her people. It took Esther's influence and power to save her people. Angie Quantrell writes that, *"After Haman convinced the king to pass an edict that all Jews would be executed, Esther found herself in the perfect position to help her people."* Here, ***"the power of one"*** is displayed beautifully. It shows that even as individuals, we are not too few to save. It took only Esther to save all. Don't be afraid if you have to be the first or if you have to be the only one to do it. Do it anyway, like Esther.

Another lesson in here for us is that, Vashti really did no wrong to have lost her position. Many observers hold her in high honour. Deen writes that Vashti is *"respected as a woman of nobility and honour who had the courage to refuse an unjust command from her husband."*

A request by her husband the king to dishonour herself deserves refusal if even he is the king. Still, she unjustly lost her position to Esther. But if you follow the story, you will appreciate why God orchestrated the removal of Vashti and the installment of Esther. A whole race of people—the Jewish race, would have become extinct had God not worked that way. While it would seem unfair in our human judgment, both we and Vashti must accept that, sometimes things must happen that way. John the Baptist had to decrease for Jesus to increase (John 3:30). Vashti had to give way for Esther to come and save the Jews. It looks like a loss to Vashti, but really, looking at the bigger picture, we can conclude that it was all good. We must try to understand things from the perspective of God. And pray that if we are occupying any positions like Vashti that an Esther needs to fulfil a divine purpose, may the will of God be done. Losses come to us all. We can get fired from our jobs and lose our positions; our marriages or friendships can break apart and our businesses collapse. Sometimes, we fall even spiritually. But God can always give us a second chance, or restore things for us.

Esther accepted the *"office"* of the Queen of Persia from Vashti as accepting destiny. It was for a purpose—to save the Jews from the wicked plots of Haman to annihilate a whole race of people. Esther risked her life for it, but fasting and prayer had gone up to God on behalf of her, by the entire Jewish race. God thus intervenes. As women in this world of dangers and fears, it must be part of our prayer to request courage and fearlessness from God to do His will, to obey Him. Esther was prepared to courageously defend the Jews against Haman—even if it meant losing her life.

Another prayer that the Book of Esther teaches us to pray is the courage to refuse wrong, no matter what it will cost us. Even if it means being deposed like Queen Vashti. Or, forfeiting our promotion, or pleasure or some other desire. The world may see it as foolishness on our part, but God will honour and reward us for it.

Esther's story teaches us about the power of combining fasting with prayer. *"Go, gather all the Jews to be found in Susa, and hold a fast on my behalf, and do not eat or drink for three days, night or day. I and my young women will also fast as you do. Then I will go to the king, though it is against the law, and if I perish, I perish"* (*Esther 4:16, ESV*). Three days of fasting and prayers had been called, and the Jews had participated fully. God is moved to deliver His people. Fasting is a powerful thing. It is a price to pay to enjoy the intervention of God in our situations. Jesus taught that some of our battles with demons and powers will not be won unless we fast and pray (Matthew 17:21).

Note also that although now a queen, Esther remains respectful and humble. *"Esther obeyed Mordecai just as when she was brought up by him"* (Esther 2:20). We learn from her that rising to power should not make us proud and pompous and disrespectful of those who helped us reach there. Many women are inclined to change their attitude and behaviour once their circumstances or status change. For instance, they are humble when they are dating—but suddenly change when they become the *"Mrs."* I urge you to pray for the grace to continue in your good attitude always no matter how high God lifts you.

Being able to speak up when necessary is crucial. You cannot pray and not act. Many women are dying in silence.

Rather than speak boldly to issues bothering them in their occupations, marriages and in the family, they swallow the pain and endure. Esther was warned by her cousin against keeping silent. *"For if you keep silent at this time....you and your father's house will perish" (Esther 4:14).* Pray that God will give you the voice to speak when you ought to speak. If Esther had not acted appropriately and spoken to the king, it is uncertain what consequences there would be. Pray that your voice will be heard and heeded when you speak.

But notice also that Esther rose to the throne, but her identity remained hidden from the king, her husband and archenemy Haman and everyone at the palace *(Esther 2:20).* If Haman had known Esther's identity and lineage, he would have devised a different plan to outwit them and eliminate the Jews. The Bible says there is a time speak and a time to remain silent. Some of us women talk too much. We do not know how to keep secrets, which is a bad thing. Ask God for discernment concerning things that you ought to keep quiet about, so that you do not bring trouble upon yourself. The moment the devil became aware of the secret to living in the Garden of Eden, humanity fell. The moment Delilah became aware of the source of Sampson's strength, he fell. We can preserve our lives and ministries and businesses and marriages by just keeping mute over certain things. Learn from Esther.

Teamwork is a powerful thing. Notice that Mordecai planned all these with Esther. The two of them so cooperated well it resulted in deep success. We must unite—in our workplaces, in our ministries and callings, in our marriages to make things work, and to win more successes. Pray for a spirit of teamwork and unity in the home, in the church, in our places of work, and in the palaces of our countries.

CHAPTER 5

Hannah

"She believed with all her heart that God was the creator of children and that only God could convert a woman into a mother."
—Edith Deen

Edith Deen also describes Hannah as the *"woman who personifies the ideal in motherhood in the Old Testament"* and her son as *"the worthy son of a worthy mother."* Hannah's challenge is not unique, but not her approach to dealing with it. There are many women in the Bible and in real life today who, like Hannah, are not *'fortunate'* enough to be blessed with the fruit of the womb. Sarah, Rebekah, Elizabeth all had problems with bearing children. I am sure even in real life, you probably know someone in your family, or church or amongst your friends or neighbours who have to face this age-old problem.

The first two chapters of the first Book of Samuel is an interesting story that teaches us a lot about going through the storms of life and how we can breakthrough. In the case of Hannah, she was not the only wife of Elkanah. Peninnah was her rival in marriage, and while the Lord blessed her womb to have children, that of Hannah was closed to childbearing. Her rival Peninnah capitalized on Hannah's barrenness to torment her. Imagine being in Hannah's shoes—seeing Peninnah always showing off to you with her children and insulting you indirectly. I believe Hannah couldn't even let Peninnah's kids provide her any service or help she needed. Elkanah's love for Hannah was deep and vivid, Peninnah and her children were very jealous of it.

Hannah turned to the Lord for help in prayer. She was persistent in prayer. Year after year at the special occasion at Shiloh, she would pray special prayers and petition God for a child. The Bible says on one of those occasions, after they have finished eating and drinking at Shiloh, Hannah stood up and prayed to God.

Every one of us have something in our life that takes the joy out of it. What is the one thing in your life that you desperately need God to fix for you? What is that desire missing in your life that gives you a reason to cry night and day? What are you doing about it? Hannah prayed to provoke heaven to release her blessing, what about you? You can also pray and demand a release of your blessings and breakthroughs. Unfortunately, many people are being lazy with their prayer life. If they do not receive instantaneous answers, they feel prayer to God is a waste of time. Are you weeping in prayers from your heart on the altar of God for a miracle? In the bitterness of her soul, Hannah poured her heart to God *(1 Samuel 1:10)*. Who are you crying out to? Where are you taking your problems, to God or to man? Or to your friends or husband? I am sure Elkanah would have so much loved to give Hannah a child if it was in his capacity to, but no, as Jacob told Rachel, husbands are not in the place of God to give children. So, dear woman, it is important to know who to go to in times of your distress.

Hannah's woes developed out of being the favourite wife. Peninnah grew jealous because of the treatment—attention and love that Elkanah lavished on Hannah. Remember Sarah and Hagar had rivalry issues, and so did the two women in Solomon's time, one of who killed her child by sleeping on it. It is good that Jesus took away this polygamous system, and thus eliminated unnecessary rivalry amongst women. I urge you, my dear fellow woman, not to allow yourself to be subjected to these treatments. Don't get into rivalry with your fellow woman, compete or fight with her over a man. Jesus has liberated women from this marital problem. Let us appreciate the liberty that Christ has offered us, and not get ourselves entangled in it again.

One negative thing we observe about Hannah is that she ignored the many other blessings and good things in her life and focused only on the one thing that she didn't have. Though she had a rival, she was the favourite wife. Her husband lavished love and attention upon her, and yet Hannah chose to dwell on the negative, and to be *"deeply depressed"* —not eating, only crying. She makes it look like life is all about making babies, which is totally wrong! As Edith Deen says, it is God who creates children, and it is God who makes women mothers. Hannah didn't have to go about sorrowful and sad as if it was her fault that she couldn't conceive. This message from Pastor Mensa Otabil goes to all men and women who desire children: *"It's important to have a child here on earth. But where we're going to spend eternity, the child you had here had no value there. We must be eternity-minded. And if God blesses you with children, thank Him for it. But don't ever compromise your faith for a child."*

After her childbearing prolonged, Rachel went up to Jacob her husband and cried, *"Give me children, or I'll die!" (Genesis 30:1)*. As a woman, I can appreciate a woman's need for children. But please, understand that children are not everything *(see Galatians 4:27)*. That is where Hannah got it all wrong. There were many people in Bible days who did not have children until they left this world. *"Michal the daughter of Saul had no child to the day of her death (2 Samuel 6:23).* Leave your ability to make offspring to God. Samuel's name means **"heard of God."** Hannah called him Samuel because she said, *"I have asked for him from the LORD" (1 Samuel 1:20).* Whatever your need, ask of the Lord, but don't be depressed and melancholy, crying bitterly because your prayer request is not granted.

In this passage, we see Hannah praying for the fruit of the womb at a time when God was also seeking for a spiritual leader for the nation of dirt. Hannah teaches us to stand out from among the crowd. She shows us how to be different and unique in a world that is going its own direction. She was seeking the face of God at a time when the entire nation had turned its back on God. In Hannah's prayer requesting for a child, she promised to give the child back to God to serve in the house of God. I believe God was so pleased by Hannah's vow because He needed a well-trained leader from birth to take over the nation of Israel as their spiritual leader. He granted Hannah's prayer and Hannah gave birth to a son she named Samuel. In fulfilment of her vow to God, Hannah gave him back to God at Shiloh to serve the Lord. Today, Samuel is regarded as one of the greatest prophets we read about in the Bible.

Many at times, when we desperately need God's intervention in our lives, we tell Him a lot of things in our prayers. We make promises conditioned on He answering our prayer, but we tend forget them. Many of us forget the promises we make to God in our desperate moments. We forget to fulfill them. Sometimes, we even forget to return to thank God for our blessing or the answers to our prayers, especially if they take a long time to manifest or if God answers them differently than we expect.

Apart from always praying for the spirit of remembrance to be able to recall what we promise God, we should also take steps to remember — such as writing them down. Have a notebook devoted to jotting down your prayer points. Put down your prayer requests or problems and lift them up to God as you pray. Then indicate any promises or vows you attach to the prayer requests. This will make you faithful to God in giving back to Him your promises.

But there are also those who do not promise God anything in fulfilment of their prayer requests. Yes, many at times, we only pray to God to give us certain desires or meet certain needs of ours. We don't add any promises or vows. Woman, rise up and pray like

Hannah and challenge God with a vow or promise. Maybe God is waiting for your promise or vow to release your blessing. He wants something from you as He wanted Samuel from Hannah. Today, decide on what you can honestly offer to God in return for the release of your blessings. Hannah prayed two kinds of prayers: first a prayer requesting the fruit of the womb from God, and second, a prayer of thanksgiving after her request was granted of the Lord. Remember to fulfil your vow to God. Remember to return and thank Him for answered prayers.

But making a vow to God is a serious thing. It is better not to make a vow to God than make one and fail to fulfill or honour it. The Bible warns strictly against that.

> *"If you make a vow to the LORD your God, you shall not delay*

fulfilling it, for the LORD your God will surely require it of you, and you will be guilty of sin. But if you refrain from vowing, you will not be guilty of sin. You shall be careful to do what has passed your lips, for you have voluntarily vowed to the LORD your God what you have promised with your mouth" (Deuteronomy 23:21–23).

Also see Numbers 30:2.

Now finally, when Hannah was praying, the man of God at that time called Eli, was watching and observing. He assumed Hannah was drunk because he couldn't hear her voice. When confronted, Hannah answered humbly that she was not drunk. She went ahead and told Eli her problem. The priest prayed for her and blessed her. Hannah's exhibition of the spirit of humility to the priest is worthy of emulation. She did not get upset by

Eli's intrusion into her moment with God. Most of us don't have patience when we are being rebuked by our pastors or the men of God in our lives. We either quit their church or speak evil about them. It pays for us to respect spiritual authority that are in our lives so that their blessings will provoke heaven to deliver our request. God wants us to obey and submit to our spiritual leaders to whom He has given the responsibility to rule and watch over our souls, and from whom He requires an account regarding how they discharge this duty (*Hebrews 13:17*).

CHAPTER 6

Anna

Anna, the New Testament's only named female prophet, lived at a time when expectation of the coming of the promised Messiah, though quite high, was held among only a few. Edith Deen describes her as *"humble, staid, serious, unearthly in spirit, a woman of a strangely expectant faith."* Deen writes that Anna lived *"aloof from worldly preoccupations"* and *"on a plane apart from material things"* and *"belonged to the godly remnant."*

The entire story of Prophetess Anna is captured in only three verses in Luke, but from this lean account, we can derive sufficient particulars about her to stimulate our desire in prayer and inspire us as women in our walk with God.

> *"There was also a prophet, Anna, the daughter of Penuel, of the tribe of Asher. She was very old; she had lived with her husband seven years after her marriage, and then was a widow until she was eighty-four. She never left the temple but worshiped night and day, fasting and praying. Coming up to them at that very moment, she gave thanks to God and spoke about the child to all who were looking forward to the redemption of Jerusalem" (Luke 2:36–38, NIV).*

This piece of scripture unveils many unique things about Anna. Although widowed, and most probably without children, Anna served God with fastings and prayers night and day. From the account of her by Luke, we can establish that Anna was a woman of great in the promise of God, who did not waver in unbelief.

At a time when almost everyone was minding their own business, only concerned about their personal life goals, she dedicated to the things of God. Anna demonstrated steadfastness in faith, being fervent in prayer, as she looked forward to the coming of the Messiah. No wonder she was one of the few to recognize Jesus, the Messiah when He was brought into the temple.

What Lessons Does Anna Teach Us?
Anna lived a life of sacrifice and self-denial. She never remarried although she had every opportunity to. (*The female descendants of Asher were believed to be beautiful, making them attractive to men who desired wives; they were Godly,*

and usually wives of priests in those days). Having lost her husband at a very young age, it was customary for another spouse to have been sought for her after grieving her husband (1 Timothy 5:14). Being a widow, Anna must certainly have had a difficult life—but by choice because she wanted to be at the service of the Lord.

Indeed, marriage was not the only thing she rejected. She rejected every earthly pleasure and material thing. She preferred fasting to food, and living and serving in the temple to living with and being taken care of by a man. This shows that to the best of our ability, we must deny ourselves certain pleasures in order to live for and please God. We may not need to choose the path of celibacy or to "not depart from the temple" but we can put God first in our choices.

Anna not only served God with fastings and prayers, she was the first to proclaim the Messiah to the world. In the temple that day of presenting the Boy Jesus that Luke writes about, Anna *"spoke about the child to all who were looking forward to the redemption of Jerusalem."*

While Naomi was bitter toward God, Anna was not. She was not bitter toward God because of her loss—otherwise, she wouldn't spend the rest of her life loving and serving Him. It was a demonstration of great faith. The faith that, even if she wanted another husband, God would give. The faith that God should have His way in her life.

Service to God is Inconsequential of Age

From Luke's description, her age is not certain. Eighty-four is mentioned, but it is not very clear whether she was 84 years old at the time of the dedication of Jesus or it is her widowhood that had spanned 84 years. But she was old, nearing her grave, and most probably, did not live to witness the ministry of Jesus which started some 30 years later. She shows us to serve God at all times—irrespective of our age. She shows us that age should not be a barrier in serving God.

The Bible admonishes us to remember our Creator in the days of our youth (Ecclesiastes 12:1). But even in our "evil" old age, we can most appropriately be dedicated to intense spirituality as we near our end or exit from this world to meet our Maker. In our old age, if we have strength, we would have lost interest in worldly pleasures. It is a time to easily overcome the temptations we couldn't overcome in our youth. This is not to suggest that we wait until our old age to serve the Lord. The Bible says the best time to serve the Lord is in our prime time—in our youth. Additionally, you do not know how long you will live. You do not know when your Maker will call you home. So dear woman, do not wait; serve your God now with fastings and prayers.

Anna points us to something peculiar to us women in our worship of God. Many women are tied to their marriages and their desires are unto their husbands as maintained in Scripture. While we must not neglect our wifely duties, it is important to not let it hinder us from devoting to God. Also, nobody should place a marital yoke around your neck, and coerce you into marriage, if even you are not called to the ministry of marriage. You are not cursed if you believe God does not intend for you to marry but live a celibate life, and dedicate your life to His service. What if God *"took"* Anna's husband just so that she could concentrate on her ministry? Being one himself, Paul encourages celibacy because we are better at serving God as singles than as married people (1 Corinthians 7:32–35). Anna exemplifies how we can devote undividedly to God as singles. She was not just a woman of prayer, but a devoted one at that.

Prayer should not be all about ourselves—*"Lord, bless me with a good marriage"; "protect me"; "bless my business and career and increase my finances"; "kill my enemies, heal my diseases"; "give me a job, visa, contract, admission."* No. We can also pray for our nation, the world, and even pastors on the field doing God's work. It is a great form of service to God and mankind. God seeks intercessors who will stand in the gap *(Ezekiel 20:30)*, and Anna was one such faithful vessel.

Many times in church or at prayer meetings, the prayer is more intense only when it has to do with our personal blessings—protection, financial breakthrough, promotion, marriage, healing. It is less intense when it has to do with the nation or church or some national issue.

I am not sure how many of us will respond to a call to fast and pray solely for our countries or political or spiritual leaders. How many of us can intercede on behalf of the Body of Christ in Ghana? How many of us are worried or bothered about the worsening spirituality in our generation? The increase in all manner of sins—pornography, prostitution, drug abuse, corruption, ritual killings? Anna shows us that our intense preoccupation with our personal interests alone is totally wrong. We must respond to the call to pray as God directs.

Anna did not pray towards a personal need. She was not serving as steward in the temple in order for God to reward her with marriage or children or financial blessings. She was praying for the fulfilment of God's promises to the world.

CHAPTER 7

The Canaanite Woman

Many women encountered Jesus during His ministry on earth. Popular amongst them are Anna, Mary Magdalene, Martha, Peter's mother-in-law, a woman crooked for 18 years, the woman with the issue of blood, a poor widow, and of course the Syrophoenician woman, also called the Canaanite woman.

The Canaanite woman is spoken of in two of the synoptic gospels—Matthew and Mark. Her story is found in Matthew 15:21–28 and Mark

7:24–30. She is the woman of Canaan in Matthew and the Syrophoenician woman in Mark. The Matthean account of her reads:

> *And Jesus went away from there and withdrew to the district of Tyre and Sidon. And behold, a Canaanite woman from that region came out and was crying, "Have mercy on me, O Lord, Son of David; my daughter is severely oppressed by a demon." But he did not answer her a word. And his disciples came and begged him, saying, "Send her away, for she is crying out after us." He answered, "I was sent only to the lost sheep of the house of Israel." But she came and knelt before him, saying, "Lord, help me." And he answered, "It is not right to take the children's bread and throw it to the dogs." She said, "Yes, Lord, yet even the dogs eat the crumbs that fall from their masters' table." Then Jesus answered her, "O*

woman, great is your faith! Be it done for you as you desire." And her daughter was healed instantly.

A simple woman she was. Not rich—because nearly all Canaanites at the time were extremely poor. By virtue of her poverty, if even her daughter's condition could be dealt with through science or medical care, she was unable to afford it. There are many things we go through in our career, businesses, marriage or ministry that money cannot solve or fix. The only avenue for permanent, lasting solution is Jesus! The Canaanite woman's prayer is a woman's plea for mercy—and Jesus showed her mercy.

The woman was not influential. She was not even a Jew—rather a pagan by religion. But she had a need: a demoniac daughter who needed deliverance. Or, a daughter *"severely oppressed by a demon."* She had heard about Jesus—and all the miraculous signs that accompanied His ministry wherever He went. So when Jesus happened to be in Syro-Phoenicia, she decided it was her opportunity to have her own encounter with Jesus— her own encounter with Divinity.

She was herself not oppressed; her daughter was. She was, as Edith Deen would put it, *"wearied in every nerve and fiber of her being by the constant care her daughter needed."* A woman who would later be described by Jesus as a woman of great faith, she took it upon herself to ensure that her daughter is attended to. She was so moved by her daughter's condition that she cried as she prayed to Jesus to come the rescue of her daughter. Love must make us able to feel what our neighbour feels. The burdens or plights of our children and relatives, neighbours and friends must be our burdens too. We must seek their relief as we would if it were us in those distressing conditions.

The woman encountered rejection and opposition. Jesus Himself seemed to be uninterested in her issue from the start. Then the disciples, assuming Jesus didn't want to attend to her, started asking Him to dismiss her immediately. Listen woman, no matter what we do, our lives would annoy other people who would not want to associate with us. The cry of the poor woman was nuisance to the disciples of Jesus, and they urged Him to send her away since Jesus didn't appear to want to help her. We just have to learn to live to please Jesus our Master, not another human being.

It is not clear why Jesus seemed to turn a deaf ear to her from the start, but this woman had her faith tested. Her situation needed urgent attention, but Jesus didn't seem to care. It is a lesson for all of us who cry out to God for help and mercy. Our faith will be tested, and it is never too late with Jesus. It never is! Many of our prayers are treated like that. Jesus often appears not to care, hear or listen. But notice that the same Jesus later commended her faith! Don't give up before Jesus commends you!

Dear woman, Jesus never turned anybody away. You will not be the first. She persisted, and was attended to by Jesus. We do not know why she received this kind of reaction from Jesus. It was the first of its kind. Edith Deen wrote, *"Nowhere in the Gospels do we find Jesus turning away from need as He did from this woman's. He did not even answer her entreaty."* Maybe Jesus knew He could use her to teach you and me how to be persistent in our faith. Because she persevered, our loving Jesus granted what she wanted, and instantly.

Jesus is a healer. Conditions that defy medication can be healed by Jesus. Situations that money, connections, social status, and family background cannot solve. What is humanly impossible for men are what Jesus desires for us to bring before Him, so that His name will be glorified. I don't know what is ailing you at this point in time in your life, finances, marriage and family life, career or health. But if you can do as this woman did—come to Jesus, kneel before Him and ask for mercy and help, you will, without doubt, have your breakthrough.

Jesus desires people who are humble—people with humble and contrite hearts. Not people who have a sense of entitlement. Notice the kind of things Jesus said to her. First, the attitude of not caring. Then He compares her to dogs, though not meant to offend her. And indeed, she never took offence. She showed humility. She didn't consider herself too important to be referred to as a dog. She was even content with the crumbs.

She cried, pleaded, went on her knees. The woman came in tears. If you need to cry, know that it is alright to cry before your Father. Even tears are prayers, too, remember? Hagar's tears were heard by God.

Like the widow of Zarephath, a non-Jew who encountered Elijah and benefited immensely from his ministry, this woman, also not a Jew but a Gentile, believed that God could have regard for her. That is why she is commended for her faith. We should never consider ourselves not qualified to be heard by God, irrespective of our background, our past, or how vile we have been in the past. This scripture is meant to teach us that Jesus has no favourites. His arms are open to all who come to Him. So I urge you, come boldly, dear woman, into the presence of Jesus and present your case.

There are many prayer requests and petitions and supplications we can present before the Lord. Her prayer was simply, *"Have mercy on me, O Lord, thou Son of David; my daughter is grievously vexed with a devil"* (Matthew 15:22). If you don't know how to pray or pray well; if you don't know what to even ask for, you can say to the Lord Jesus, *"Have mercy on me, please." You can kneel before the Lord and say, "Lord, help me."*

Persist in your prayers, and in your faith. Too many people give up on God too quickly. Don't stop until Jesus answers your prayer. You may have been praying the same prayer a long while now without receiving your answers, but don't stop. Perhaps you started praying and believing God for your answer before others started praying. They may have received their answers before you but don't you stop praying.

Again, we learn the habit of intercession from this woman. The Canaanite woman was petitioning Jesus on behalf of her daughter. Dear woman, your children need your constant intercessory prayers. Your husband needs your intercession. Bear your family up in prayer without ceasing.

ABOUT THE AUTHOR

Mavis S. Agyemang is a pastor, author, healthcare professional, wife and mother. She was ordained into ministry after graduating from the New England School of Ministry, Connecticut, where she obtained a Certificate of Ministry.

Reverend Mavis A. Agyemang is also a certified professional nurse, and has accumulated over 20 years of experience in the healthcare practice. She is the author of Daughter of Zion; and co-author of Spiritual Horns.

A devout Christian, Mavis is a mother to many in the Lord. She is a proud

alumni of Accra Girls' High School.
Mavis is happily married to Franklin
A. Agyemang, with whom she lives
in the United States with their four
children.